CHANGING
OF THE GUARD

An Encounter with
the Spirit of Manipulation

KASHA HUNT

KO PUBLISHING
FORT WORTH, TX

Contents

Foreward

I was introduced to Kasha Hunt over a decade ago and I knew God's hand was on her life. She embodies charisma, power and most importantly, genuineness. Kasha is a great teacher, eloquent speaker and now an amazing author.

As I write this foreword to her captivating and informative book, *Changing of the Guards*, I share words that I always hoped I would have the chance to write. Kasha Hunt is not just serving as Executive Pastor in my church, she is an amazing gift to the body of Christ; creative and committed to sharing truth. Her experiences are shared with a purpose of reconciling people to the kingdom of God in a way that only she has been anointed to do.

One of the things lacking in the body of Christ is transparency. Oft, people say everyone can't handle your testimony; and although this can be found true, the people God assigned to you can. The book of Revelation 12:11 NLT tells us, *"And they have defeated him by the blood of the Lamb and by their testimony."*

This book shares much wisdom and insight into the spirit of manipulation; how to overcome, be healed and restored from it. This book is a must-read.

Evan D. Risher
Lead Pastor
Ramp Church Texas

Acknowledgements

First, I want to thank my parents for pushing me to succeed. What an amazing set of parents I have been blessed with, Pastor J.L. Hunt Jr. and Cheryl Thomas. To my siblings, family and friends for your continuous love and support.

Many thanks to my spiritual Father, Overseer Evan D. Risher and my spiritual Mother, Pastor Yvonne D. Bennett, Detroit, MI. You both have been instrumental in my spiritual journey and I am eternally grateful. Mother, my Mentor, your spiritual advice and tutelage has been invaluable. Overseer, I will never forget you left the ninety-nine to come after me.

To my church family, Ramp Church Texas, you have encouraged me through it all. I will forever be grateful.

To my late Grandmother, Rev. Phyllis Louise Shy Johnson, I dedicate this book to your memory. You are the wind beneath my wings.

x

"A Spiritual Journey"

CHANGING OF THE GUARD

"A Spiritual Journey"

When I was an adolescent, I went from Barbie's Dream House and Corvette to purchasing Romance Novels at garage sales while perusing with my Mom. Harlequin, Silhouette, whatever I could get my hands on. It got to the point where I was finishing two books a day.

I couldn't get enough of the magical world of romance, where Prince Charming comes in and sweeps the Lady in Waiting off her feet. I wrote my first romance novel at the age of 13, it was only 25 pages front and back, but it was a reflection of this fact; no longer were these books simply entertainment, better yet, I had caught the vision enough to write my own.

I must admit that although my reading expanded my vocabulary immensely, widened my internal dictionary and

"A Spiritual Journey"

matured me in the ways of romance; it also filled my head

with apples and cinnamon when it came to relationships.

Throughout my years of failed dating and broken

engagements, no one ever fit the cookie cut idea I had of a

romantic relationship. I desired romance above all else.

I wanted the man in the books, but the reality is it doesn't

happen like that for everyone. And the truth is every fairy

tale, on the outside, is not indicative of the inside.

When I look at couples today, everyone's story is different.

Some met in High School, were High School sweethearts

and married soon after and are still married today. Some

dated for 5 years, broke up 16 times and then got married. I

don't know of many that have my story, and if you do, I'd

love to hear it.

I met my husband on a Wednesday Night at a Bible Study,

saw him at church the following Sunday and started chatting through social media about the church.

The next time I saw him was three weeks later, on a Thursday evening, that Friday he helped me Christmas shop. Saturday, Christmas Eve, he proposed. The very next Saturday, New Year's Eve, we were married.

Of course, there are other significant spiritual things that happened in this four-week time frame that we will get into a little later in the book. But, if I had to put it into a nutshell, that would be it.

A lot of times we experience things in life, good and bad, and we totally miss the spiritual meaning because we don't realize *'Everything'* that happens is part of God's plan for our lives. We don't want to believe that God planned or allowed tragedies in our lives. It is easier to believe that he had his hand in all the good things, the Victories, the

Triumphs.

We don't want to imagine God angry or disappointed

because it doesn't fit our picture of God, the humble dove.

Yet in the Bible He shows himself as a jealous God, a

punishing God, and a God that teaches through trials.

When you accept God in His entirety, it makes the trials a

lot easier. It was this reality that I had to face many years

ago, and this same reality aided me in my process.

This book is a testament and chronicling of God's infinitely

woven plan that was set into place before the foundations

of the earth.

Selah

"The Journey"

CHAPTER ONE

"The Journey"

I grew up in a Christian home, my Father *(Preacher)*, Mom, three siblings and a dog. Yes! I was a Preacher's Kid. To confirm some of the rumors that preacher's kids are the worst, I will say that the attack is even greater on kids of parents in Ministry.

The enemy delights in causing havoc in the homes of those who share the gospel. The enemy desires to use whomever he can as a distraction. It's kind of hard to focus on preaching on Sunday when your child is rebellious and disobedient.

This is just one of the many D's that the enemy uses to keep us from reaching our fullest potential. There's a total of five (5).

"The Journey"

Deception

Distractions

Disappointments

Discouragement

Discontentment

When I look back, I like to think my childhood was akin to the Huxtables. Well, that's always the point of reference I use when describing my family growing up. I had a great childhood, straight A student throughout Elementary and Middle School; educated, loving parents, beautiful home, and an amazing family.

In High School everything kind of changed for me, it was a turning point. One decision changed my life forever, some would say it changed the course, but, hard as it is to believe, it was part of God's plan.

"The Journey"

It is mind blowing to know that even our mistakes can point us in the right direction. Therefore, it is such an integral point to understand that when God says he forgives us and throws our sins into the sea of forgetfulness to remember no more, that He is not holding our past over our heads.

'His forgiveness wipes the sleight clean!'

We are the ones that don't forget. We don't forget our own transgressions nor the transgressions of others. This is very unfortunate because it leaves no room for the possibility of forgiveness or change.

It is easy to say with our mouths that we are a work in progress, but we harden our hearts to anyone outside of us that does not fit our idea of where everyone in Christ should be.

"The Journey"

The Bible explicitly says, "Judge Not, Lest Ye Be Judged", yet we judge people every day. We judge the Pastor, we judge our Brothers and Sisters, we judge our family members, we judge the homeless; we act as if we were all ordained judges.

Even the most spiritual have judged behind closed doors. How do I know? Because I've been behind those doors. Listen, this is not to chastise anyone, everything God put in His word 'not to do' was put there because He knew we had the propensity to do it.

One thing I was constantly being told was to stop being so hard on myself. Come on, I know I am not the only one. We know there is therefore no condemnation to them that believe, but we condemn ourselves or we allow the voices of the enemy to bring condemnation over us.

Conviction is from God, Condemnation is not!

Don't get me wrong, I am not an advocate for sin, and sin separates us from God. It's God's redemptive blood that gives us the freedom to pick our heads back up and keep pressing!

Let me tell you, for me, when I gave my life to Christ, I didn't magically become a Saint. At that moment my processing began. I'm still in the process.

People have set unrealistic expectations of Christians. We are working to be more like Christ, we are NOT Christ. We are riddled with imperfections, which is why the gold process is used so often to describe the Christian Process.

Gold Process – Gold in its impure stage is placed in a melting pot over temperatures up to 1000 degrees. As the gold melts, the impurities begin to float to the top and the gold maker uses a scraper to skim the impurities off the top.

"The Journey"

The gold boils until no more impurities rise to the top. It is a tedious but worthy process.

History says that Gold was first discovered and used by the Egyptians in Egypt and Mesopotamia in 3500 B. C. They would mine the gold from stream beds and use the gold to create elaborate jewelry, religious artifacts, and utensils like goblets.

Just like gold, God allows us to go through fiery situations to burn off our iniquities. To purge us of our impurities. But like fire, it's not comfortable, it doesn't feel good but it's necessary.

Tell yourself, 'It's necessary'.

I tell you God really impressed this in me during my journey. How even the worst things in life that happen to us are necessary.

"The Journey"

Is it fair? Not to us. Is it justified? Not to us. We should remember that we are not our own, we belong to him. That was one of the hardest things for me to do, lay down my will for His.

We grow up with our own expectations out of life and out of ourselves. In Elementary we are taught to choose a career path when our teachers ask that age old question, *"What do you want to be when you grow up?"* For those who didn't have an answer, we were made to feel unstable and unsure.

This question was meant to stir up our portion of faith that nothing is impossible to them that believe. However, we take things too literal. There were some careers that were off the beaten path; like wanting to be a movie star, an author, or a musician. Those were considered unattainable goals to some and children were often encouraged to pick something more practical.

But to God be the glory, even though we were taught to stay in the box, there are those of us who came into the knowledge of who God is and what it means to be His.

We realized we could blow the roof off and all the things that were deemed unreachable or unattainable are now being accomplished.

As a child, I wanted to be a writer. I aspired to be a fiction writer. What happened to that dream, that seed, how did it get buried? What distracted me?

Think back to when you were a child, what made you happy? What made you feel accomplished? How did you lose it or what replaced it? Maybe you accomplished it!

"The Journey"

It's funny, my whole career has been in Accounting which is the opposite of a fiction author. One works in specifics and the other fantasy and fairy tales. I'm here as a witness that It's never too late to pick up where you left off, to go back to school, or to learn a new trade. To begin to dream again.

"Don't ever give up on your dreams."

Get it in your spirit, if I can think it and believe it, I can achieve it. Honestly, during High School I got so off track. I made horrible decisions.

As a Preacher's child you would think I should know better, you would think I knew God and that I would be on the right path but to be honest, I was distracted.

After being coddled and sheltered my whole childhood, remember I was a PK *(Preacher's Kid),* I literally lost

"The Journey"

myself once I smelled the scent of freedom.

"I was already free in Christ;

I just didn't know it yet."

As parents, it's important that you allow your children to have a well-rounded existence. My family was very active, we travelled, I was exposed to different cultures, different cuisine, the works. Unfortunately, we always want what we can't have. Not realizing that we are so blessed.

Most of life is spent chasing after what we don't have and not much is spent enjoying what we do have.

I've learned to take the time to smell the roses, but at what cost? I often asked over the years, if I could do it over again, would I choose differently? I've gotten to a point in my life when I realize *I had to go this way.*

"This road led to my destiny!"

"The Journey"

As messed up as it was, as dark as it was sometimes, as crazy as it was, my story was written before the beginning of time. Who would I be if I had gone a different way?

Would I be further in life, would I be as bold, would I be this tenacious, or would I be worse? Only God knows and to be honest, it really doesn't matter. All I have is now, this moment, and I can't get it back once it's gone.

Throughout my adult life I've lived all over this nation, from Los Angeles to Las Vegas, Atlanta to San Diego and down home to Texas and I must say that I give God praise.

My journey has taken me on some highs and lows. I've been prosperous and I've been abased. I've had it all and lost it all. I count it all joy. Like Paul, I've learned in whatever state I am in, therewith, to be content. To be thankful.

"The Journey"

I look back on all the scenarios in which I could have been sleeping in my grave, but God! He had plans for me and he has plans for you. You did not go through all you went through just to exist. There is more for you.

I wasn't always in this head space. I have had suicidal thoughts, suffered from depression, stuck in addiction, committed fornication, cheated in my marriage. I have been a thief, a liar, you name it and I was that. I may not have physically murdered anyone, but I've murdered their character with my tongue.

I'm not speaking to you because I have always had it together, but God is using me because I kept getting back up. God says in His word a wise man falls seven times and gets back up.

Pray for Wisdom.

"The Journey"

What makes him wise? He keeps getting back up. God never promised we wouldn't fall; he just wants us to keep getting back up.

You lost a loved one, get back up! You just lost your home, get back up! Don't stay down there.

"For He knows the plans He has for us,

to prosper and be in good health."

Jeremiah 29:11

I must admit that each time I get back up I'm stronger. Some of the things I've endured others haven't recovered from. This book would not be readable if I tried to tell it all. It would be a collegiate sized textbook. Half of it would be filled with my trials but the other half would be giving God glory for His goodness and His mercy. I made it!

I wanted to lay the foundation by giving a little of my history so you can understand what happens next.

"The Downfall"

CHAPTER TWO

"The Downfall"

Romance was such an integral part of my life from a teenager on. It was the reason my marriages failed, the reason my relationships didn't last, the reason I was unable to be content with average or normal. I never knew that relationships required work and sacrifices and selflessness.

The romance books didn't talk about it, the romance movies didn't show it, and nobody sat me down and gave me the real deal Holyfield. All I had were my childhood memories of what it should be like and unfortunately, nobody could meet the standard.

Throughout High School I dated and even had some relationships, but they didn't last because I was looking to be courted but they were too young to even know what that looked like and were probably never taught what it meant. This made it hard for anyone to hold my attention for long.

"The Downfall"

I was always looking for the next best thing. Even as an adult, I had a list of requirements and expectations and if you didn't measure up, I wouldn't even consider you. I was married at the age of 22 to the love of my life.

At 22, I did not know what it meant to be a wife. He was my best friend and he was my husband but what was I? I tried to do everything that the women did for the men in all my research; candle lit dinners, sexy lingerie, romantic interludes, I had romance down.

However, I lacked in other areas; like how to listen, how to meet his other needs, how to be a good Mother to his daughter, how to make our house a home.

He had his own ideology based on his experiences being raised with a distracted Father. As a child his Dad would take him to other women's house and swear him to secrecy, so he saw the husband as a cheater and a liar.

"The Downfall"

He witnessed his Mother being severely abused by his Father and so he saw a husband as an abuser. He saw his Father as the provider who ruled the household and so he sold dope so that he could provide. I was the wife I thought I should be, and he was the husband he thought he was expected to be.

We are products of our environment.

During our marriage I suffered abuse, but like most women in abusive relationships, they tell themselves it's not that bad, it's not that often, it will get better, he's just mad, he's just jealous.

I really thought one day soon he'll realize how much I love him, and the abuse will stop. I can't lie, I was down for a minute but after one year of dating and nine months into the marriage, I got up and moved back to Texas.

During that season I went through a gamut of emotions. I was hurt, downtrodden, self-conscious, I felt ugly, I felt like I couldn't do anything right. I know what it is to love and be in love with someone who scares you, intimidates you and abuses you.

Trust me my Sister and my Brother, you can get up. You can live without them. You can put your life back together. I left everything and had to start over. Even though I didn't have a personal relationship with God he was still with me. Even then.

Since then my first husband has changed, he's no longer that man and we are still friends to this day. I see him every time I fly to Los Angeles.

From that time forward, every gentleman that I entertained would always try to tie me down. I had one gentleman refuse to take me home from a date until I said that we were boyfriend and girlfriend. You're laughing but I am serious. Not one relationship lasted.

At the age of 32, I was engaged to a very sweet man who stole my heart. I wasn't expecting it, I wasn't looking for it, I just needed another man on my volleyball team. He came in, helped take us to the Championship and we won!

Initially we would talk after practice about the game and about God. It was so refreshing to be able to speak to someone who knew God, who loved God and who had experienced Him. There are a lot of surface Christians out there but it's different when you connect with someone that has a relationship with God.

He asked me out and we began dating. He knew a little something about romance. Because remember, that was all that mattered to me at that time. I had to be romanced. That was my love language.

"The Downfall"

Our first Valentine's Day, in lieu of a dozen roses, he gave me a dozen reasons why he loved me. He cooked an elaborate meal, candles and all that lovey dovey mushy stuff that I needed.

During our Volleyball Championship game, we were in the last period, last play of the game, game point and we had possession of the ball and he calls a time out.

Everyone went crazy, the other team because they were gaining on us and had finally caught up and my team because he wasn't even the coach. I was!

I start asking him is he alright, is he hurt, trying to figure out why he stopped the game. He was acting so weird, more than usual. Then finally I get surrounded and I notice that all my family start coming out the stands towards the court.

You can imagine, during a championship game, energy is high, adrenaline is flowing. I'm ready to play and prayerfully win! Game is tied.

This is for all the marbles and I turn around and he is on one knee with a ring asking me to marry him. And the cameras start flashing and immediately I'm transferred into this surreal fairy tale where I have on a ball gown and he is dressed like a Prince and I say, Yes, and curtsy!!!

This is it you guys. It was what I had been waiting on, Mr. Perfect.

When he proposed I really felt like I could spend the rest of my life with him. It was not until later that I realized, I may have acted too hastily. I was blinded by romance when something was amiss. I couldn't put my finger on it, I couldn't even describe it but there was something off.

"The Downfall"

We started attending his church together, I grew up Baptist, he grew up African-Methodist Episcopal. I was willing to convert. We counselled with his Pastor, and I was duly preparing to move my membership to the AME church after the wedding. The closer we got to the wedding the weirder things began to get.

There was an outside influence at work, and I started to put two and two together. If you don't know, most women are natural private investigators.

The pieces were adding up one way, but I didn't want to believe it because I was so close to having what I always dreamed of. The most romantic, affectionate, sweet, handsome man ever. Did I say fine?

I need to add that he was a sculpture. A work of art, DaVinci could not have done better.

"The Downfall"

I deserved him, after all I had been through, I deserved to be happy. I got on my self-righteous stage and began to come against what I knew to be true because of what I wanted.

Women always think, I can fix him. Truth is, some things only God can fix and if you go into a relationship with that mindset you are destined to fail.

"But I wanted what I wanted."

One month away from the wedding, things are semi-good, but there's this underlying issue; you keep disappearing, you are not in place most of the time; but when I'm with you I feel like I'm the only one in the world.

I was struggling within myself, with myself, between what I knew to be right and what I desired more than anything, to be in a romantic marriage with my Prince Charming.

Three weeks away, the truth could no longer be ignored. I had to stop fooling myself and accept the fact that no matter how much I desired it to work, I could not marry him.

I'll never forget the day I came home to change clothes for an event, and he was waiting for me outside. He had never looked so attractive; I'm talking Denzel Washington attractive. It was hard but I had to tell him that it was over. The wedding was off.

Later that evening he knocked on my door. I went to the door and listened to him beg me to please let him in. He apologized profusely and my heart melted but I didn't open the door. I had never feared him before but there was fear on me, I wore it like a coat.

After 30 minutes of talking through the door he asked me for some water and I said 'okay, meet me at the front door' and as I was opening the door to give him his water, he came around the side of the house and to me he looked like a demon.

I hurriedly placed the water on the ground and closed the door. He never picked up the cup, he was never thirsty. He wanted me to let him in.

I kept telling him call your Pastor, call your parents, there's nothing I can do for you. I even encouraged him to call my Dad or my Mom because my heart wept for him.

He sounded so hopeless but every time I would move towards the door, I would see bullets and knives coming through the door, so I never opened it. I wouldn't even stand in front of it. Eventually I told him I was going to bed and I would talk to him in the morning, I begged him to go to his parents' house.

"The Downfall"

That was the last time I ever spoke to him and the last time I heard his voice. God put me in a deep sleep. The next morning his car was parked in front of my house, but I didn't see him in it. I thought, he must have walked somewhere as I got ready for church.

After I was dressed and ready to go, I got in my car and as I passed his car, I noticed a water hose in his gas tank, and I was shocked to see that it looked like someone had syphoned his gas.

As I drove to church a bad feeling began to come over me and by the time, I had made it to my Dad's church, I was literally shaking. I explained to my Dad what had happened the previous night and what I saw when I left.

I begged him to please come back with me to check on him and the car.

"The Downfall"

My Dad, I love him so much, he simply asked someone to preach for him and drove me back to my house. My Dad got out and checked the vehicle and confirmed my worst fear, he was in the car. His gas was not siphoned, the hose was going from the exhaust pipe into the car.

He had killed himself, in front of my house. He died from asphyxiation. When my Dad told me, I let out a wail that can't be described. I felt as if my heart was being ripped from my chest.

I held my chest as if I was having a heart attack. I had never felt anything close to this searing pain. I began to sob uncontrollably as he called the police and we waited.

While my Dad was speaking with the police, I remember saying, *God help me*, over and over again. I knew he was the only one that could.

"The Downfall"

A small voice said go and see him, as the police had left him in the car as they spoke to my Dad a little further down the street. I felt like I had to see him just one last time, to say goodbye.

It took me forever to get out of my Dad's car and when I finally did, I could hardly walk. I could hardly see through the tears as I headed for his car, but my Dad caught me midway crossing the street, before I could get to the car. He spoke gently to me and said, *'you do not want to see him like that'*.

The small voice was the enemy, he wanted me to have that picture etched in my mind forever so he could play it back repeatedly. He is the tormentor. God would not let it be so.

During his funeral preparation and services his family acted like they didn't know me, they blamed me. If it was up to them, the world would never even know that I existed.

"The Downfall"

I wrote a poem which I read at the wake, that epitomized him; he was always smiling and laughing, he loved music, he was a saxophonist, he had travelled the world playing professional soccer, he was amazing.

His Pastor, who had been counselling us, who was mentoring me, who was preparing me to be in Ministry at his church, called me up to the front at the funeral to read that very same poem I read at the wake.

You know how the bible speaks of how the first shall be last and the last shall be first? Here me and my family were at the largest AME church in the city, moved from the front two rows all the way to the back row, which was almost 20 rows back.

I remember sitting on the back row looking at the program disheartened, not one mention of me, pictures of people that he didn't even know were listed as friends. Not one picture of us.

This whole illustrious full-sized in color 12-page program listing every accomplishment, every award, every family member and every friend and not one mention of me or my family. My family which took Carl in and accepted him as one of them, my family who loved Carl, helped Carl, nothing. My heart was so broken.

When I was called to the front, I had to walk past every one of them and when I finally arrived at the front of the church and stepped behind the podium everyone else had used, his Pastor gestured to me and called me up even higher.

I walked through two levels of steps into the pulpit, which had even more steps before getting to the mic.

"The Downfall"

I stood in that pulpit and I announced who I was and what I was to Carl. You could audibly hear the intake of breath echo in the room.

His Father was high ranking in the City of Fort Worth and so the police, fire department, Mayor, City Manager, and city workers were in attendance and all of them were shocked at my existence.

I unfolded my heart in the form of a single piece of paper and before reading it I thanked his family, his church family, and his Pastor for loving me. Lastly, I thanked my family for loving him and I read my poem.

I read it while tears streamed down my face. I read it past all the pain, the disappointment, and anger. I read it all, the serious parts, the funny parts, and everyone that knew him concurred with my anecdotes.

"The Downfall"

When I concluded I thanked his Pastor for allowing me to read my poem and walked the long trek back to my seat. Even though I was left off and out of everything related to his services, God saw fit for me to say goodbye in my own way.

"God will do what only he can do."

We left the sanctuary after the family and guests and as I descended the church steps his Mother was waiting for me. She came up to me and asked me to ride with them in the limo to the Repass and I passed on the opportunity. I politely said thank you, but I was still reeling from the hurt and rejection experienced at her hands.

I couldn't help thinking to myself, you told me I was the daughter you never had, you said we were family. I felt accused and betrayed.

"The Downfall"

It was months later that God showed me it was meant to be a murder/suicide. My fiancée planned to take my life and then take his own. That's why God kept showing me knives and bullets coming through my door. It explained why I didn't hear him in the backyard getting my water hose from under my bedroom window.

When I tell you that God has kept me safe in some situations, He has kept me! I'm sure you can look back over your life and recall times where God preserved your life. Accidents, abusive situations, wrong place wrong time situations; yet you are alive reading this book today.

Even after this tragedy, I still desired to get married.

One day, not to long after, my Sister-in-law came to me and shared a dream she had about me. She dreamed that I was walking and there was a man and he was all blue, from his head to his feet, no facial features, and he was trying to entice me to come to him.

As I kept walking there appeared another man and he was all red, and he too tried enticing me to come to him. As I continued there were more men, each a different color than the last until I finally reached one that was all black.

This one began to tell me things I've always wanted to hear, he was more cultured than the rest, more savvy, more eloquent and more cunning. He whispered in my ear every good thing and with him I went. She told me to be careful because the enemy was going to use men to distract me. Me in my naivety took it more literal.

I was intrigued with the dream and thought these men were indicative of the men in my past. What I didn't know was they represented what was ahead. It wasn't until years later that I understood what that dream meant.

"The Downfall"

After this prophetic dream I was proposed to three times by three different men in a years' time. Men that I hardly knew and had just begun dating. These weren't fly by night proposals; they were well thought out, romantic and sincere.

One of them did it in front of my whole family on Christmas Eve after only three months. I was opening my gifts and I was encouraged to open his. I went through the whole box in a box in a smaller box until I got to the ring box. By the time I was ready to open it he had positioned himself in front of me and asked me to marry him.

My nieces and sister went crazy and all I could do was stare at the ring. I didn't know what to say, I didn't know him. My mouth stood agape as I eventually said yes, but my heart nor my mind was in it. Needless to say, it was a short engagement.

"The Downfall"

Just as God knew my desire, the enemy knew my desire

too. He was trying to figure out how he was going to get

me. I was trusting God more, I had stepped into the

ministry, I was learning more, growing, the enemy desired

to sift me as wheat. Oh, but God prayed for me that my

faith would not fail.

"The Guard"

CHAPTER THREE

"The Guard"

I'm one of those women who always wondered why they would seemingly *always* end up with wrong guy. The liar, the cheater, the psycho, the lazy one, or the one that tears you down. You know the type.

The Liar – he can't tell the truth for the life of him, he tells unnecessary lies and when there's no need for a lie, he lies. He lies about his past, his present and his future. He thinks impressing you will keep you, not considering when the truth comes out.

"No relationship built on a lie can last."

You want someone you can be honest with and eventually reveal all your idiosyncrasies to. I am not saying on your first date announce that your struggling financially, you got two baby daddies, you hate your food to touch, you can't cook, you have an addiction to Xbox, you're lazy and you have a gas problem. Some things need to be revealed as you get to know a person more, but don't lie about it and cover it up. It is what it is.

Some women will wake up before their mate, put on makeup, and get back in bed. Some men put socks in their underwear to give a false impression. We are living in a time when individuals are creating illusions of who they are.

I am at the point in my life, if you can't love me for me, then this is not going to work. I can no longer become what you want me to be, because if I'm being her, who's being me?

The Cheater – he refuses to be faithful no matter how good you are to him. You can have his dinner prepared every day

"The Guard"

when he gets home, dressed in lingerie, smelling and looking good, wash his clothes, keep the house clean, have his babies, attend his events all while looking fabulous, and he still cheats.

Or she can't be faithful even though you give her flowers just because its Tuesday, you run her bathwater with candles around the tub and rose petals floating in the water, you massage her feet when she's tired, pay for her hair and nails, take her on romantic dinners and excursions, pay the bills and yet, she just can't keep it together.

The truth is some people are not ready for commitment but like the benefits of being committed. They like the perks but have no intentions of being with one person.

Some of us, when it's discovered we've been cheated on, look to ourselves for the reason, but your truth may be that it's not your fault. You had absolutely nothing to do with it. Some people cheat because they like the thrill of it. They either like the hunt, the danger or the scandal.

The Psycho – this person is crazy for real. I'm talking busting windows out of cars, burning clothes, disrespect your Mama, slashing tires, hiding in bushes, putting trackers on cars, the popping up on you type.

The psycho, 9 times out of 10 is dealing with insecurities. It's hard for them to imagine that they got you. And because it's so unimaginable they have to believe there is someone else.

They are so convinced of their truth that everything is overwhelmingly blown out of proportion. It's so unfortunate that a simple discussion can lead to an argument that results in them holding a knife or a gun threatening to take your life because they can't imagine living without you.

Most of their stories are made up and developed in their own mind. On the flip side, some psychos are created through lying, infidelity and illusions that you created.

The Lazy One – this one is tired all the time. Too tired to take the trash out, too tired to make one of your football games, too tired to go out, too tired to cook, too tired to help around the house, too tired to pick your Mom up at the airport, too tired to watch the kids. You find yourself asking people outside of your relationship for help and the first thing they ask is, what about your wife or husband?

The lazy one refuses to put any effort into the relationship, whether friendship or romantic. You find yourself doing all the work, making all the contacts, conducting all the communication, by yourself. The lazy ones add wear and tear to relationships. The truth is if you are making all the effort, they are not interested.

In addition, there are the spiritually lazy. Yes, you can be lazy spiritually. When someone is trying to live right or do the right thing it's sometimes easier to go with the flow of the flesh.

It takes an effort to resist temptation, it takes effort to talk yourself down or fight your own will. Some are too lazy to fight and give in to temptations rather than resist.

The Tear Down – this one refuses to celebrate anything with you but will point out every error and every mistake. Always quick to say what you should have done and how you could have done things differently. Will talk to you non-stop for 30 minutes about their accomplishments and then when you try to share your day and how good it was, they cut you off and bring up another topic centered on them.

The ones that tear you down are selfish. Since it's not about them and it's not bringing them glory, they have to minimize you so that it doesn't overshadow them. You may say, I just got accepted into the Master's Program and they'll say, how long before you get your Doctorate?

They can't just celebrate you where you are, they always must one up you to make you seem smaller than you really are.

I used to cry out to God, when is it my turn? When will I truly find love, when will I truly be happy? Because to me marriage equaled happiness. I believed I would never be complete until I was married, had a family, a white picket fence, the two-car garage, and all the other stereotypical things expected.

"The Guard"

I thought my match had finally found me. It started out as a business relationship. He rented an office from me and we started to try and do some business together.

It was challenging work and Lord knows I love a challenge. We started making strides, I was enjoying myself immensely, not even noticing that I'm doing a lot of work but not seeing any of the money.

I looked at it as investing my time with a reward later. I invested myself so much in his business that I began slacking in my own and ended up losing a government contract. This resulted in me working full-time with him. I don't blame anyone for my failures, I accept full responsibility. I got distracted.

That's why it's imperative that we stay focused, *stay woke* as they say. I didn't and I found myself working *for him*, while he called it *with him*, and we grew his business quickly and immensely.

I later found out that his whole adult life he always had a woman for everything. He had a woman that helped him with his kids, a woman that would help him with business stuff, a woman that would assist him administratively and he slept with them all. He had never met anyone that was capable of being every woman, until he met me.

Throughout our relationship we had many up and downs. Most of them were due to his ideology that for the rest of his life he would need to be in a relationship with several women to meet all his needs.

This joker imagined that they would all live in the same home and no one would be jealous of the other and they would be one big happy family.

"The Guard"

He wanted to be a polygamist. With African American women? What planet was he from?

I had my own ideas; I was going to show him that he was certifiably crazy. All he needed was me. And I turned into Superwoman and he believed it, for a time.

> *"Once you lower your standards of what*
> *you will accept and what you won't,*
> *you open yourself up to all kinds of nonsense."*

I went through some things with him. Isn't it crazy that individuals that cheat always think your cheating? Late night pop-ups, crazy phone calls, showing up where I'm at will make one go crazy. So, I got just as crazy as him. Can I just be transparent?

I created a fake Facebook page and became his friend. Yes, I did! I couldn't get any concrete evidence otherwise, until one day the office phone rang. There was a hysterical woman who was asking me to come to one of his rental properties because he was trying to put her out.

My first reaction was, why are you calling me? Then she said there were some things I needed to know. That was all she needed to say, me and my girlfriend hopped in the car and drove to the property where she began to tell me her tale. She told me how for the last year he had been dating both of us.

I listened and realized she knew everything about me; she knew we worked together, she knew what car I drove, she knew where I was Christmas and Thanksgiving, she knew dates and times, she began to lay everything out. All I could do was listen.

I was looking for evidence, second-guessing myself, doubting what I knew to be true and I guess God said this girl just doesn't get it. It was made very plain and undeniable. Naturally, he denied everything. His excuse? She was jealous of our relationship.

Why is it when men get caught cheating, they refuse to own it? I'm sure women do to. I feel if you are big and bad enough to cheat at least be man or woman enough to admit it. Of course, our relationship ended. How do you come back from that?

Even during it all, God was answering my prayer. I didn't want to marry a fool and He kept me from doing just that.

"As Christians the world will test us,
they will try to cause us to doubt our intuition, doubt what
God is saying and showing, for their benefit."

Let every man be a lie and God's Word be the truth. What is his Word - He is the Word. The Bible says in the beginning was the Word and the Word was God. When he speaks to us, we must not allow anyone to cause us to doubt. Once again, I believed what I wanted to believe, but because I asked God to reveal the truth, he did it as only He can.

How many of you have ever asked God to reveal something and what He revealed was exactly what you thought it was? We have something innately built in us called discernment, some call it *Mother Wit*, others intuition.

"He is a revelatory God, he created revelation."

God saved me from myself…again. You would think at this point I would have given up on ever finding true love. However, those romantic images were so engrained in me, they were part of me. I didn't feel complete without them, without the desire.

So, I kept praying, God he's not the one. Send the one, let him find me. I know you're hiding us from each other. Nevertheless, your will.

"The Guard"

We are so quick to tell God, nevertheless Your will.

Truthfully, we are hoping that His will is our will. We're

like God I want this so bad, it's got to be your will.

Unfortunately, it doesn't always work out like that.

It took me forever to realize that until I lay down my will it

will be impossible to receive His will!

"The Last Guard"

CHAPTER FOUR

"The Last Guard"

God called me into the ministry at the age of thirty-six. I was licensed by my Father/Pastor and during my licensing service I literally felt the weight of ministry on my shoulder. It was so heavy; I could hardly stand during the ceremony; I ended up falling to my knees.

I don't remember much of the verbiage from that day but the one thing that has always stuck out to me was when my Father said, *"after this, no turning back"*.

Those words slammed me in my chest; I can't turn back, there's nothing back there. Most didn't know how significant that was to me because they were unaware of my past. They didn't know about my struggles with addiction, my fights with self-esteem issues, my suicidal thoughts, and my relationship issues. But God!

"The Last Guard"

If you looked at my history, I would be the last person that you would think God would call. My friends and classmates were surprised that I accepted my call into the ministry. I was the rebellious one. The adventurer.

Mouths dropped when the word began to spread. Kasha Hunt, a Preacher? Are you serious? Kasha Hunt? You know it's bad when they say your name twice. I had a reputation, I was known as the class skipper, the one in trouble, the drug user, the drug dealer, the gambler, the heart breaker, etc. I was even affiliated with the Rolling Sixty Crips while living in Los Angeles. I thank God that my past did not disqualify me.

"God calls the Unqualified."

I began ministering for God; laying hands on the sick and seeing miracles in person. I transitioned from God telling me to do something and me giving Him all the reasons I shouldn't, to actually trying it and seeing His glory be revealed. Even in witnessing this there was still part of me that didn't feel worthy of the Call. Just as we intellectualize the disciples walking with Christ, God in the flesh, and witness them still having faith issues.

Truth is, we are just like them. We see miracles every day but let a light bill be past due or we receive a bad report from the doctor and our faith goes out the window.

God is looking for a faith filled generation that truly believed him in John 14:12 when he said, *I go to be with my Father but the things I have done you shall be able to do also, and even greater things than these.*

Even though God said it, we still have trouble believing that we have power through Christ to make the lame walk and the blind see, even to raise the dead from the grave.

During this time, God began to show me how mighty he was and over time I began to feel strong in Him and confident in my Calling. It was a call, I didn't ask for it, honestly at times I didn't even want it.

I want to encourage you today, if God can take this ex-gangbanger, ex-drug dealer, ex-drug addict, ex-fornicator, and ex-party girl and use her for His Glory, He can use you.

Don't allow the enemy to persuade you otherwise. It doesn't matter what your background, all He needs is your willingness. Do you have a "Yes" in your spirit? I said yes and it was the best decision I ever made. Yes to your will, yes to your way and yes to your assignments.

When I met my ex-husband, I was on fire for God. I felt I was strong and happy in Him. I didn't feel as if I was lacking anything. I met him at my Father's church and as I told you at the beginning, it was a swift courtship.

Ironically, I was not interested. I was in a relationship with another preacher; now this *Man of God* must have gone to Courtship school. He was the epitome of a gentleman; thoughtful, romantic, and fashionable. Did I say romantic? He hit all the marks on the checklist, tall, confident, self-sufficient, dark and handsome.

He was what women call a Classical Beauty. This means a man that is so handsome he's beautiful. We were dating pretty heavy. Travelling, candlelit dinners at the finest restaurants, gifts, surprises and more.

I was in love with him, but it was a relationship that was filled with promises of commitment and marriage that never came true. Be aware of individuals that are conflicted within themselves and vacillate.

"A double minded man is unstable in all his ways."

"The Last Guard"

Then I met my ex-husband, let's call him Beelzebub.
That's what I called him after it was all over. What I didn't
tell you at the beginning was how it was orchestrated.

He reached out to me on social media to talk about my
Dads' church, eventually the conversation turned, and he
began asking me about me. How was I feeling? How did
my day go?

I found myself rejecting him daily in my DM, but it was
like he had insight into me, insight into my struggles, my
doubts, my fears. Eventually I gave him my number. It was
like he could read my mind and really see me. He would
speak my thoughts. How did he know?

He knew what to say, how to say it and what to say it
about. That got my attention. Not many people take an avid
interest in you or try to interpret you or see into you. He

could read my thoughts. It was true intimacy – into Me you see.

Even when I told him I was dating someone he did not care. He would constantly say that my friend wasn't the one for me and tell me all the reasons why he was. I guess he wore me down because I finally agreed to see him. During this time of conversing with him I broke it off with my Preacher friend.

I ended up inviting Beelzebub to an opportunity for a network marketing business. After the meeting, we went out to eat and had a really good time.

I want you all to know that I was NOT head over heels in love with him. It was never my intention nor was it made up in my mind to date, much less, marry this man. I hardly knew him, I'm not foolish as most thought I was.

I previously referred to some spiritual occurrences that influenced my decision-making process. Here we go!

On Christmas Eve we were on my couch just talking about God and His goodness. As we got deeper in our conversation, I jumped up and ran in the restroom because the spirit of God had come over me and I didn't know how he would react.

I remember being in my bathroom and my spiritual language took over and I was consumed by His presence. Have you ever tried whispering in tongues when the Holy Spirit is moving? It's impossible. He must have heard me!

I eventually went back into the living room and there he was with tears in his eyes and God spoke to me and said he's going to ask you to marry him, say yes. And lo and behold, with tears streaming down his face and shaky hands he reached towards me and he asked me, and I said yes.

"The Last Guard"

I had dreamed of this moment my whole life. Someone that God approved of, someone who understood me, loved me unconditionally, a sweet, romantic, handsome, and intelligent man that most of all, loved God.

I truly believed it was God ordained and the very next day, Christmas. I announced it to my family. Even in their shock they were supportive.

My Mother and Sister-In-Law were miracle workers. They organized the whole wedding and we were married the following week on New Year's Eve in Downtown Dallas at Thanksgiving Square.

It was a beautiful wedding, wedding dress, bridesmaids, decorations, photographer, the whole deal. That first month after the wedding was bliss. Then things began to shift, almost immediately.

"The Last Guard"

Tomb of the Unknown Soldier, guards are changed every 30 minutes during the summer and every hour during the winter.

The tomb is guarded every minute of every day since 1937

"Changing of the Guard"

CHAPTER FIVE

"Changing of the Guard"

I married my dream man, but it wasn't until two years later that I would realize he was the man from my Sister-In-Law's dream that was black from head to toe. He was the one that would say all the right things but have the darkest soul. He was on assignment and the crazy part is it wasn't a demonic assignment, God told me to marry him.

We started off as most newlyweds; giddy, goofy and in love! I would look forward to coming home from work. I was very understanding as he had moved from Dallas to Fort Worth. I understood that he would need time to get adjusted and find employment. I understood that he was starting over. I knew that his number one desire was to take care of me. How? Because that's what he consistently told me. So, I went to work every day while he looked for work.

"Changing of the Guard"

On the weekends he would go over his cousin's house and I was excited about being around his family. They would hang out, head to the back. I was enjoying the moment, but it didn't take me long to realize that something else was going. I soon discovered that they were doing drugs in the back.

As an ex-drug dealer and user, I noticed the telltale signs of white power around his nose, I noticed the constant sniffing and extra energy. They would go outside and come back in and I would smell the stench of marijuana, but I just sat there.

I allowed him to believe that I was oblivious to what was going on, knowing that no manner of cologne or air freshener can cover up the pungent smell of weed. I allowed it. I didn't stand up to him, I didn't say this is not acceptable in our marriage, I said and did nothing. This just made him bolder and eventually they stopped hiding and began doing it in my face.

It was disrespectful but I didn't see it as such. I was in love, he was romantic, and I thought, I'm okay with his flaws. Everyone has them. As long as I stay saved, at least I'm no longer fornicating, I'm married now. I'm legitimized by this legalistic process and can no longer be convicted. This is what I told myself.

Truth is I didn't say anything because I wasn't as delivered as I thought I was. It's easy to maintain deliverance when there is no temptation. I had been clean for years but truthfully, I wasn't delivered. I just didn't put myself in positions to be tempted.

I stayed away from the old places and the old friends. You know you are truly delivered when the thing that had you bound has no effect on you, you don't want to see it, don't want to be around it, you despise it.

I saw nothing wrong with what he was doing because I wasn't truly free from it. That's another thing I gained in my two years of HELL, true deliverance!

"What you don't confront you can't conquer!"

Eventually, I found myself asking to hit the blunt, next it was Ecstasy, which I never had tried before, but he promised me it was only a sexual enhancer. I still hadn't realized what a manipulator he was.

Months passed by and he became the victim who could not find employment. It was societies fault; he was a black man with a record that couldn't find a job.

"Changing of the Guard"

According to him he went on multiple interviews a day and never received any call backs. Turns out he was not even a convicted felon. This was one of the many lies that he used to manipulate me in the marriage.

I sympathized with him, I mourned for him, but the truth is he never wanted a job, he was content hanging out every day. He would even go as far as driving by places saying they are going to offer me a job, I start Monday and Monday would come and there would be always be an excuse of how they did him wrong or lied about the position and gave him a reason why he couldn't start. I had never met anyone that would go through so much trouble for a lie.

Most men very rarely show emotion, my ex-husband, was the most emotional person I had ever met. Male or female.

"Changing of the Guard"

He was explosive, a bully, a cry baby, easily hurt, easily offended, quick to misinterpret. My whole world, which was built on a solid foundation began to crumble. Everything I was sure of became unsure, everything I believed in became confused.

I was attending the best church in the world and my husband did everything in his power to pull me away from the church. He embarrassed me at my Dad's church to the point he was no longer welcome and then he stole money from my home church and moved me to Dallas.

I was so caught up in the emotionally charged situation that I let down my guards and that is how I began to start smoking weed again. I found peace from the chaos there. He loved it; he did his best to keep me high. Pick me up from work with a blunt, get home, here's a blunt, time to go to bed, here's a blunt. My subdued mind made it easier for him to weave his web of lies on me.

There is a big difference between a liar and a manipulator. A liar tells lies to cover something up or prevent from telling the truth. A manipulator tells stories and acts out their lies to change your reality.

A liar will say I looked for a job today. A manipulator will meet you at the door in anger throwing papers around and having a tantrum because no one called them back for the job they never applied for.

He was always the victim and I found myself apologizing time and time again for things that he had done to me. Don't get me wrong I had met manipulative people before, but he was on another level of manipulation. He had the spirit and it was strong. I had no clue who or what I was in covenant with.

"Changing of the Guard"

The biggest manipulation was with our money. I would give him money to pay something, like our storage, while I was at work. I would look up and there would be a note saying my storage is being auctioned off and I would say, Hey! Why didn't you pay for the storage? He would begin yelling and throwing a fit saying how I know he's not working and how he needs things too.

So, I lost all my childhood memories, my furniture, clothes, etc. because you don't have a job? It didn't make sense, but it would end with me apologizing to him.

In two years of marriage we went through four vehicles and two apartments and one home, all at my expense. Over the period of our marriage he may have worked a total of 8 weeks and I never saw a dime of what he made. He tried to call himself a drug dealer, but he used more than he sold.

I'm not trying to portray myself as the victim, I am just painting the picture.

He was mentally and emotionally abusive. His favorite thing to call me used to be "Baby Girl" and then it shifted to "Coward". He would get in my face and tell me what a coward I was repeatedly.

This went on for months. Initially I wanted to punch him in his face but as time wound down, I began to believe I was a coward.

I was so worn down that for a season of six months I literally was a zombie. I would go to work and get off work and not remember one thing I did that day. He would talk to me and I would just stare into space. I was very mechanical, no emotions. I believe it was a safety mechanism that took over to keep me from losing my mind.

"Changing of the Guard"

I thought I had been in jealous relationships before, but this was another level. I couldn't come out the house when he wasn't there, I couldn't be on the phone because he was too insecure.

We would be grocery shopping and he would yell at some random guy, "Hey, why are you looking at my wife." Ready to fight at grocery stores, parking lots, stop lights. I was living in HELL!!

I couldn't even wait in a line without someone looking at me and him feeling like he needed to check them. And then if I gave him a look like 'dude chill, you are embarrassing us.' He would start yelling, *"Oh what, I'm embarrassing you. I don't care"* and he would continue to yell and try to fight whomever.

"I truly began to hate him."

Then, as if the emotional and mental abuse wasn't enough, he eventually began to physically abuse me. He busted my lip and I had to get stitches; I still have the scar. He busted my head and I had to go to the hospital, yes, still have the scar.

He was intent on tearing me down until I was nothing. Throughout our marriage it never dawned on me that he could be on assignment, I was too busy asking God why he would place me in this situation. Crying and praying for help to get out, praying for grace and mercy, praying for a way of escape. *He was on assignment.*

In addition to all this craziness my husband was obsessed with the Illuminati and a lot of conspiracy theories like reptilian people, aliens walking among us, etc. So, what did we do all day and all night? Watch videos. Video after video replaced the real God. Theory after theory replaced faith until I was consumed as well. And for a season in our

marriage, my God was YouTube.

"Anything you put before God becomes your God."

"Year One"

CHAPTER SIX

"Year One"

The first year of our marriage God showed me, Me! Before
I got married, I thought I was perfect except for the few
times I fornicated. I really thought if and when I get
married, I will be perfect. Au Contraire'!

In that first year God showed me how selfish I was, how I
would ask people to do things for me that I wasn't willing
to do for them. He showed me how unappreciative I was
for family and friends. I took a lot of things for granted and
it wasn't until I was pulled away from my family, my
church family, my Pastor, and my friends that I began to
truly value those relationships.

Then when my material things were lost, I realized how
much value I placed on what I owned. Until I was shown
how quickly I could fall back into sin I didn't realize how
religious I was and not spiritual.

"Year One"

I loved God, I preached, I taught, I laid hands but had no real personal relationship with God. I didn't know Him intimately, if that makes sense. I was the image of a Christian but the strength that I was operating in was my own, not His!

I had to acknowledge that I was not a wonder and people weren't blessed to be around me. I had such a reality check. *The Man in The Mirror* is no joke.

We focus so much on superficial things, as long as we look good, we are good! We may be full of bitterness, heartbroken or disappointed but all we care about is how people see us.

If I have my hair snatched and my makeup flawless, the right clothes, the right shoes, I'll be alright. No one will know I'm dying inside; no one will know I'm having thoughts of giving up and checking out. No one will even think to ask me if I'm okay because I look Fabulous!

Truth is 9 times out of 10, this is true. The bible says, *'those that are spiritual restore them'*. I was broken, I was disappointed, I was hurt, I was 'wooking pa nub' in all the wrong places and nobody could see it. And the crazy part is I didn't even know it.

I really thought I was tight with God, like we were aces. I felt spiritually strong before my marriage. Yet I found myself falling back into drug use, being manipulated, and allowing someone to pull me from my relationship with God.

What a reality check! I wasn't all that and a bag of chips. I was not the best thing since sliced bread. I was not as deeply rooted in God as I supposed. I thought I was unshakeable until someone shook me. I thought I was unbreakable until someone broke me.

In a million years I would never have thought that I would be where I ended up in just two years. Broke and disgusted. I was the bad turned good one, I was the one that could preach and teach. Me!

"We have to be careful of haughtiness because God has a way of bringing us low."

Thank you, Lord, for waking me up! That first year showed me all my flaws and I discovered them in the fire.

The fire was the emotional and mental abuse. God will use the weirdest thing to plant a seed.

In year one my husband would call me selfish and I would take the stance of how dare you. I'm perfect now that I'm married.

"Year One"

The seed began to take root and grow, and scenarios began to roll across my minds movie screen and God showed me the times when I displayed selfishness.

If someone close called me and said their car broke down and they were stranded, my first reaction would be to ask, "Well, who have you called?"

Immediately I would begin recommending other people they should call first before me; I would tell them use me as a very last resort. Call me after you have called everyone in your Rolodex.

Then God would show me when my car broke down, my little Sister would get up at 5:30 am to make sure I get to work in Irving by 8:00 am. Yet, I couldn't even get out of bed or turn the food off I was cooking to go and pick her up stranded on the side of the road. God replayed many movies.

"Year One"

My Mom is my biggest advocate, my greatest supporter, anything I've done or wanted to do she was right there to help make my visions come true. You would think I would do anything for her but nope.

If it inconvenienced me, I would say I wasn't available. I would make up excuses of why I couldn't go somewhere or do something.

Now, I want to be inconvenienced. I want to serve. I want to be there for my family, but I had to be shown myself. During this year of revelation God showed me so much about myself I was literally transformed. He had to tear down those walls, break up that fallow ground so that the well could be dug.

When we look at the Samaritan woman at the well. When Jesus asked her for a drink, he told her that He had some living water in which you will never thirst again. The woman asked for that water and Jesus said, where is your husband? Before he could give her the water he had to deal with her fallow ground; he had to prepare for the well to be dug in her that would sustain the living water.

She answered, I have no husband and Jesus said, you're telling the truth. The man you are living with is not your husband. Truth is you've been married several times.

The woman was astonished and wondered who is this man that knows all my business. She said you must be a prophet; she had no idea that He was more than a prophet.

Before God could give her the gift, he had to dig the well. My first year of marriage God dug a well in me so when he truly poured His living water in me it would hold.

Those of you from the country or you know about digging a well can attest that digging a well is hard work. You must dig it deep, but as you are digging you must fortify the walls of the well to keep the walls from caving in on each other. God was digging and fortifying. Through the name calling, the manipulation, the revelations, the tall tales and loss, he was digging and fortifying me.

I never knew how materialistic I was. I really felt that what I owned and the car I drove reflected how important I was and how chosen I was. I had to have the best cars, the best house, the best clothes, the best shoes, I was a true consumer. I wasn't saving anything because I had to have everything.

I was a shopaholic but it's nothing like good ole' poverty to break a cycle. I was used to buying what I wanted when I wanted it. Since the age of 18, I've worked and went to school. I bought my first car; I rented my first apartment.

"Year One"

My grandmother taught me good work ethics. She was an Entrepreneur most of her adult life, a millionaire over and over again. Have it, lose it, have it again!

I loved working, I loved using my mind and I mostly enjoyed getting that paycheck every week. Money was power to me. I didn't have to put up with anything in relationships because I had my own.

It was easy for me to walk away from people and things because I felt I didn't need anyone. God had to show me that I needed Him!

I need you Father!

Those nights when I laid in my bed crying out to God, asking Him to please help me. He was showing me, money can't get you out of this, material things can't get you out of this, you need Me!

"Year One"

During year one there are so many things I discovered about myself.

Begin to ask God to show you yourself so that you can be what you think you already are.

"Lord let us see what you see."

"Year Two"

CHAPTER SEVEN

"Year Two"

The second year of our marriage God showed me him. The first year I had no idea I was being manipulated, I believed everything he said, I went through the emotions with him, I cried with him, I got angry with him, what he said made sense, but in year two a light came on.

I began to see how he weaved the webs. It was a meticulous process. He had such foresight; he was such a planner. The manipulation would start days, sometimes weeks before the finale!

I had never met someone so intentional. It was like watching a movie or a play that was scripted with the end already known by the lead character.

I began to see how the random stories told today would fit with the stories told the day before or next week.

"Year Two"

One incident in particular comes to mind. I remember coming home from work one day and when I arrived, he began to rant and complain about people breaking into cars in our neighborhood and what he was going to do when he caught this person.

He was very detailed on specifically what he was going to do, and I wondered, why is he so upset about these break ins, we weren't robbed? Sure enough, two days later I asked about my camera and he goes into this story of how our car was broken into and he thinks he knows who did it.

He takes off out the house to go around the corner and jump on the person he thinks did it. The whole time he is gone I'm thinking to myself; he pawned my camera. Why go through all the theatrics?

Things became clearer to me as time went on. He tried to control absolutely everything so he could control my perception and my reality which he wanted to be the distorted world that he created. I began to see through the deception, but the Holy Spirit would keep me quiet. He would get so angry when he began to feel that I no longer believed him. This discovery could and would lead to violence.

The biggest and last method of manipulation was convincing me I was pregnant. It was impressed into me so strong my belly even began to grow and I began to have symptoms. The mind is such a powerful thing.

Our belief is so powerful. I truly believed I was pregnant for months. It wasn't until I went to the Hospital and they confirmed I was not pregnant that I finally stopped believing. I never forget sitting in the hospital hallway with my Mom grieving over the lost child that I was never impregnated with.

"Year Two"

I am not giving this spirit any glory; God gets all the glory,

but I want you to understand how it operates so you can

defend yourselves against it.

Psychological pregnancies (pseudocyesis) are a real thing.

Some of the symptoms are:

- Missed periods

- Swollen Belly

- Weight Gain

- Swollen Breasts

- Morning Sickness

- Sensations of fetal movement and contractions

I had every symptom but the morning sickness. He would

use the baby against me at every turn. Every day, the baby

this, the baby that. The crazy part is I knew I wasn't

pregnant at the beginning but after weeks of months of

hearing about the baby I began to feel life in me, I would

"Year Two"

feel flutters, we would put our hands on my belly and feel it

together and in these moments, there was false hope. Hope

for something better between us, hope of salvation, hope of

reconciliation.

The biggest asset to being pregnant was it distracted him

from all the other foolishness and for once, I had a reprieve.

Once I discovered the pregnancy was not real, I shared it

with him, and he literally told me:

> *"I don't care what the hospital said,*
> *You're still pregnant!*

How arrogant and bold he was to make such a statement,

and the prior year, sad to say, I would have fell for it. But

this was the year God was revealing this spirit to me.

This was year two, the Changing of the Guard.

"Year Two"

I read an article in Charisma News that described the spirit of manipulation to a tee.

"It is almost like a spell (or witchcraft, to be precise)!

I discovered that people with issues of control never let go of their power easily; they would rather sacrifice their relationship and ministries rather than give up control; because having control, in their perspective, is their greatest payoff. Manipulators do it for their own satisfaction, they could care less about the person being affected.

Here are some signs that you are in a manipulative relationship or being manipulated by someone.

- *The manipulative person never allows you to prove your point in an argument. They control the conversation to avoid losing the argument. They will over talk, yell until you give, keep interrupting or resort to theatrics. They cannot stand the idea of losing their position of power over you. They will twist things around or go down a whole different road that has nothing to do with what you are talking about to avoid losing the argument.*

- *The manipulative person will use temper tantrums and threats to control you. You will see them go into fits of rage and throw temper tantrums when they can't get their way because they will do anything, even to the point of violence, to have their way and manipulate you into obeying them.*

- *The manipulative person will constantly try to make you feel guilty or bad about the way you are treating them when the truth is, they treat you horribly and should be apologizing to you.*

"Year Two"

Even though they may be the abuser they will make the abused feel like they are the abuser by using reverse psychology. This way they are able to fool the naïve one they are controlling into believing the abuser is the victim. In turn, the real victim ends up apologizing and the abuser continues to abuse and control them.

- *The manipulative person always expects more from you and is never satisfied. Another way they control you is making you feel that nothing you do is ever good enough, that you always fall short. This makes you feel indebted and obligated to try hard to please and satisfy them. Truth is no matter what you do it will never be enough. They want you to feel as if you are failing.*

"Year Two"

- *The manipulative person will always question your motives. By continually questioning your motives, you never can be sure of yourselves and therefore you are always on shaky spiritual and emotional ground. This could cause the victim to look at the manipulator as a role model to be looked at for godliness and purity, which puts them in their place of control.*

- *The manipulative person is always putting you down. This is another form of controlling you. Calling you names (like coward), questioning your decision-making capabilities. This can make the victim feel obligated to try harder to please them and trust their wisdom, so you end up letting the Controller make all the important decisions because you no longer trust your own ability to*

make a sound decision.

- *The manipulative person has to have their way.*

  Unlike a healthy relationship of give and take; the

  manipulator is always working to have their way.

  You may have a say in minor things like

  where to eat, but major decisions, like where we

  live or what we drive are made by the manipulator.

- *The manipulative person will walk away from their*

  responsibilities as a way to manipulate others. They

  will walk away at the worst possible time if they

  don't get their way, therefore, almost blackmailing

  you in a sense to let them have their way. They will

  put you in a horrible position by threatening not to

  attend an important meeting or refusing to allow

you to go somewhere important. This causes the victim to acquiesce in order to avoid being embarrassed or missing work or an important engagement. This method is a very common form of control.

- *The manipulative person will find a way to impose their will in every situation. Their goal is to force their will and agenda in every meaningful situation. Ultimately, they get their way!*

- *The manipulative person will continuously threaten to end the relationship. Especially in a marriage or dating situation, they will threaten divorce or to walk away from the relationship once they realize that you will cave in. They use this as a way to get what they want even though they have no intentions of going anywhere.*

- *The manipulative person will threaten to commit suicide. If they feel threatened or if they need attention or care or if it will get them their way, they will make the threat. In most cases, they will never kill themselves if given the chance, but they will play on your emotional strings to get you to give in to them to stop them from going through with it.*

- *The manipulative person will withhold physical affection. Often women will withhold sex to manipulate the man into giving in to their will. This method doesn't work too well with women as they are not always as sexually motivated as men,*

"Year Two"

however, a manipulator will use whatever weapons

he/she identifies works.

To manipulate is to negotiate, control or influence for one's own advantage. One thing we must know about this spirit is it does not travel alone. Satan loves to deceive which is why it's so vital that we pray for discernment.

> *"The spirit explicitly says that in later times some will fall away from the faith, paying attention to deceitful spirits and doctrines of demons. Such teachings come through hypocritical liars, who consciences have been seared as with a hot iron."*
> *I Timothy 4:1-2*

Demons allure people from a position of stability into a place of instability in an attempt to capture them in their web of lies.

I was in such a low place in my life that I would rather leave this earth than remain alive in this marriage.

"Year Two"

Most people would say, *just leave*. That is the ignorance of our society that thinks a woman or man in an abusive situation can just walk away.

Bigger than the physical abuse and the emotional abuse is the web that is weaved in the abused mind. Ending a significant relationship is never easy. It's even harder when you've been isolated from family and friends, psychologically beaten down, financially controlled, and physically threatened.

A woman is not going to meet a guy that beats her and just hang around for more. There is so much more that goes into it. The abuse starts in the mind long before he puts his hands on her. You see in an abusive relationship, the man *IS* the victim, which leaves the woman no room to be the victim or vice versa. They must now become their abusers Savior.

"Year Two"

We begin to make excuses for them. *He hit me because he was abused as a child, I'll save him. He only hit me because he thought I was cheating; I'll show him I'm not a cheater and that I love him.*

There are so many reasons why men and women abuse others. There's even a reason why they abuse their children. There is an underlying message that comes across that it is the victim's fault and they are completely innocent. If only you wouldn't have done this or did that. They play the blame game.

I'm here to tell you that you can successfully get free! I want to speak to someone that may be in the process of making the decision to finally leave an abusive relationship.

- *If you're hoping your abusive partner will change -*

The abuse will probably continue to happen. Abusers have deep emotional, psychological and sometimes spiritual issues. While change is not impossible, it isn't quick or easy and it can only take place when the abuser takes full responsibility for their actions, seeks professional help, and stops blaming you, his or her unhappy childhood, stress, work, their habits or their temper.

- *If you believe you can help your abuser -*

It's only natural to want to help your partner, you love them. You may think you're the only one that understands them or that it's your responsibility to fix their problems. But the truth is that by staying and accepting the repeated abuse, you are reinforcing and enabling their behavior. Instead of helping, you're perpetuating the problem.

"Year Two"

- *If your partner has promised to stop the abuse* -Abusers often plead for another chance, beg for forgiveness, and promise to change. They may even mean what they say in the moment, but their true goal is to stay in control and keep you from leaving. Most of the time, they quickly return to their abusive behavior once you've forgiven them and they're no longer worried that you'll leave.

  - *If you are worried about what will happen if you leave*

You may be afraid of what your abusive partner will do, where you'll go, or how you'll support yourself or your children. Don't let fear of the unknown keep you in a dangerous, unhealthy situation. The longer you can stay away, the stronger you will become.

"Year Two"

I never forget one of the fights me and my first husband

had one evening when I was running late from work. My

car kept overheating so I would have to pull over and let it

cool down. There were no cell phones back then, only

pagers. I'm telling my age!

When I finally got home in Pasadena, he had gone to take

his daughter back to her Mother in Los Angeles and by the

time he arrived home, I was fast sleep. I was awakened by

hands around my throat choking me, as I fought for my life

he finally let up before I passed out and said *if I would have*

just come straight home, this wouldn't have happened.

A normal person would have asked why were you late?

What happened to you? But he wasn't normal, he wasn't

raised normal, he was a by-product of abuse in his

childhood home. The blame was always shifted to me.

"Year Two"

Just like in my first marriage, I prayed for change. Like most victims of abuse, they pray to God to change their partner.

We know that God is an absolute gentleman and that He will not force His will on anyone. We are deceived into thinking this person really wants to change, so we pray accordingly. We will even pray with them. Yet in their heart, they're thinking you are the problem not them. How do I know if they truly want change?

Helpguide.org article listing *"SIGNS that your Abuser is NOT changing"*:

- ✓ *They minimize the abuse or deny its seriousness*
- ✓ *They continue to blame others for their behavior*
- ✓ *They claim you're the one that is abusive*
- ✓ *They tell you that you <u>owe</u> them another chance*
- ✓ *They say they can't change unless you stay*

"Year Two"

✓ *They try to get sympathy*

✓ *They expect something from you in exchange for them getting help*

Once a person has been mentally trapped the physical prison is easier to maintain. Just like every prison there must be a guard, the abuser now becomes the guard.

It's a gradual take over, using subtle techniques but it has been accomplished time and time again.

Most use fear as a Controller, some use mind tricks and others the victim mentality. My ex was the worst, he used all three. You know they say hindsight is 20/20 which is true in some cases but in this relationship the Holy Spirit had to reveal the height, width and depth of my tormenting relationship.

"Year Two"

"The Holy Spirit revealed how through manipulation I lost everything at the very moment I felt I was the strongest."

In year two it all began to come together. God unraveled me myself and showed me and then showed me the oppression I was under. I stated earlier that the spirit of manipulation aka Jezebel does not come alone.

The ___lying spirit___ was present. This spirit manifests in strong deceptions, flattery, religious bondage, false prophesy, accusations, slander, and lies. Beelzebub was filled with this spirit as well. He took on a false spirituality during our marriage, mostly everything he spoke for a season was heard directly from God. *God said* was another weapon used to control.

The ___perverse spirit___ was present. This spirit manifests in evil actions, filthy mind, doctrinal error, sex perversions, pornography, twisting the Word and foolishness.

Beelzebub had such a perverted mind, not just sexually, but in all aspects. He perverted God's Word and would try to convince me I had learned it wrong all along. He proceeded to pervert our bedroom with pornography and lust.

The ***spirit of haughtiness*** was present. This spirits manifests in arrogance/smugness, pride, idleness, self-deception, rebellion, self-righteousness, and rejection of God. Beelzebub was narcissistic. He always talked about himself, he fantasized he was successful and powerful, he believed he was superior, he required constant praise, he had a huge sense of entitlement, and he took advantage of others.

The ***spirit of bondage*** was present. This spirit manifests in fears, addictions (drugs, alcohol, cigarettes, sex, etc.), compulsive sin, and bondage to sin. Beelzebub was in bondage in every aspect of his life. He was under satanic influence and succumbed to multiple addictions. Some

would call it addictive behaviors but it's the spirit of

bondage.

Those were the spirits I was able to identify in year two

when the Holy Spirit began to bring revelation. There could

have been more, just unrevealed.

"The End"

CHAPTER EIGHT

"The End"

If I be honest, all of us can manipulate a situation to work in our favor. A Woman in a relationship with a nice man discovers that when she pouts, she can get what she wants; so, she starts pouting to get more of what she wants. Or the little girl who has Daddy wrapped around her finger and can get whatever she wants if she says the right thing, the right way. That's manipulation but it's not the spirit of manipulation. There's a difference.

As our marriage wound down, we moved from Dallas back to Fort Worth and were staying in Extended Stay Hotels, which was very costly and of course, all on me. He was abusing alcohol and drugs daily by this point. One evening while having an argument, he headbutted me and blood began gushing out of my head, right above my eye. He panicked and tried to hurry and leave the room. He was

very afraid. It was only the second time I had seen him like
that.

Abusers act like they are not scared of anything, like
they're crazy, but I tell you who they are afraid of, the
Police. He was so afraid I was going to call the police that
he ran out with hardly any clothes on and fled the scene in
my car.

While I waited to see if he would return, I began to pack
my things. This was the beginning of the end. I called my
family and asked them to pick me up the next day. He
returned the next day and of course, I was gone.

He immediately started the manipulative phone calls. He
was so sorry, it would never happen again, just come back.
Not once did he say how are you, did I hurt you, are you
okay?

"The End"

Not to bore you with every minute detail but we were separated while he was supposed to be seeking God and counseling. He lied about that too!

It finally ended when I last saw him. This encounter resulted in him busting my ear drum while socking me as hard as he could in my head. He then ran into his room and came back with a microwave and proceeded to throw it into the windshield of my car. For those of you that need closure; I did press charges.

A few months later he was arrested in the process of purchasing drugs. He was charged with possession of a controlled substance.

When he arrived at his arraignment he was presented with the new charges and he plead guilty to domestic abuse and was sentenced to two years in prison. During his incarceration I filed for divorce.

"The End"

I had returned to my church and I was weak and broken.
My spirit was broken; I was defeated. Week after week
God began to restore me, little by little. He meticulously
began reconstruction and began putting all the pieces back
together again.

I was struggling with accepting what had happened to me.
Mostly with knowing that God told me to marry Beelzebub
knowing what evil he was capable of and secondly, I
struggled with no one believing God would tell me to do
that. I began to get confused in my mind, terrified I had
missed God so badly.

That same year I was at the altar during service, crying,
bent over, a shell of myself and my Bishop was in town. He
sidled up to me and whispered in my ear, *God Allowed It*!

When he said it, my spirit quickened and I cried like a
baby. It was such a release that took place. To know I

hadn't missed God, it was the Lords doing. I held fast to those three whispered words by S.Y. Younger.

When I would come under attack from people that didn't believe God would allow anyone to suffer, I remembered *God Allowed It*. When I began to doubt in my own mind, I would remember, *God Allowed It*.

It would be years before I would understand the fullness of what God was saying through my Bishop. It would be many sermons, personal devotions and discussions later before the magnitude was revealed.

The following year our church was in consecration and I was late to prayer. My Pastor advised me the altar was still open. I quickly made my way to the altar and I began with exaltation, then I proceeded to pray for the list of things in our prayer focus.

"The End"

As clear as day, I heard God say, *Give Me Marriage*. It startled me initially because it was such a random request. Did God just say, Give me Marriage? What did that even mean? After my initial shock I obeyed and I opened my mouth and sincerely told God, *I give you marriage* and immediately something broke.

I began to weep like I was mourning a death. I cried from my soul until my eyes were almost swollen shut. It was a guttural cry, just me and God. I felt like something was ripped from my inner being but afterwards I felt such a lightness. There was a heavy weight that was removed from me when I offered my personal sacrifice to God.

As my dreams of romance and marriage burned and became the incense of a burnt offering that flowed upwards to heaven, I felt God and all of heaven smile! I went through all that, for this.

"The End"

It was in that moment that I realized that my desire to get married was a weight, it was a form of bondage, a stronghold. I was bound by that desire. I couldn't have healthy relationships with men because I was obsessed with it. I couldn't meet someone from the opposite sex without imagining us getting married.

Strongholds cause reoccurring destructive behaviors.

My ideology of romance was a stronghold; albeit one that kept me from being married 17 times. I never felt so free. When I rose from the altar, I was physically lighter. I gave God marriage at the altar on that day and I walked out a free woman. Free in my mind and in my Spirit.

Two years later when Beelzebub was released, he called me, texted me and sent pictures every day for four to five months straight and to this day he randomly reaches out.

"The End"

He was unaware that the spell had been broken; all his words of adoration were lost on me. I never answered the phone, other than the first time, nor responded to any texts.

It's crazy how someone can be so attractive when you are in love and then downright ugly when you see them for real.

That spirit was so confident that it just assumed that I would fall right back in line. Silly rabbit! During that two years of his incarceration I had got back in right standing with God, my family and my church.

I began living again. I got a new strength. I was strong in my own might before, now I was strong in His might. He showed me He was my fortress, my shield, my strength, my peace and my joy!

"Things I Learned In The Fire"

CHAPTER NINE

"Things I Learned In The Fire"

It wasn't until two years after my divorce that the Holy
Spirit gave me the full revelation of my experience with the
spirit of manipulation.

> *"It was good for me that I have been afflicted; that I might
> learn thy statutes.*
> *Psalm 119:71*

All my whispered prayers of God I want to be more like
you, I want to love like you, I want to be used by you, use
me for your Glory. He says, this is how you get my Glory.

I have to tear down everything you built up against me,
every high place must come down. I have to dig up your
fallow ground so I can access your well and pour in my
living water. I have to tear down your pride and show you
that you are nothing without me. I must allow you to see

your enemy in a personal way so that you can help others combat this spirit.

This spirit is destroying the church, it's destroying careers, families and marriages. The spirit of manipulation is running rampant in the world perverting everything to convolute the Truth.

"This spirit is strong, even the saved, sanctified and Holy Ghost filled can become subject to its wiles."

God can't address what is not recognized and exposed. We need to reevaluate our prayers. Are we praying for and against the right things? Most of the time we are asking God to change a situation when we may need to be praying against a particular spirit. Learn them that labor among you translates to discern them that labor among you. Discern their motives and their intent.

Be wary of those who speak everything you want and need to hear; for the enemy hears your moans and complaints and speaks them into the ears of them that carry this spirit. This is how they know what areas you need help in or are lacking and they become that.

The spirit of manipulation is an offspring of Jezebel. In order to understand the spirit of manipulation we must understand Jezebel.

Jezebel in the natural was a biblical character possessed by one of Satan's demons that rebelled against God. The spirit that possessed Jezebel was many, legion. She was married to King Ahab.

Jezebel and Ahab work as a team and normally where you find one you will find the other. They enter our lives through the gate of bitterness and unforgiveness.

"Things I Learned In The Fire"

Some of Jezebels Characteristics that often pass unnoticed:

Fear *– this spirit inspires fear in men. Fear paralyzes us in both the exercise of our spiritual gifts and our freedom.*

Intimidation *– this spirit uses threats, blackmail or peer-pressure to keep people quiet. Fear of being hurt or humiliated paralyzes many and leaves them totally unable to act.*

Abuse of Power *– this spirit abuses its power to get what it wants. Because it is influential it uses its influence to subtly manipulate people. It's a spirt of control, of servitude and manipulation.*

Division *– this spirit will ignite tensions between husband and wife, brothers and sisters, children and parents. Jezebel works diligently to separate*

129

people. It is like a hurricane leaving destruction in its path. Families are destroyed, churches are finished, best friends become great enemies.

Mockery *– this spirit likes the assembly of gossipers. It will use the people with big mouths to mock church and family members, discredit the local assembly and discourage Christians. Jezebel pushes its victims to leave the assembly or even abandon the faith.*

Calumny *– this spirit spends its time spreading poison over others. It enjoys criticizing others and staining them with insults. It gets joy in tearing others down.*

Defamation *– this spirit is a false accuser. Defamation is an accusation or an imputation of a fact that brings dishonor to a person of morals.*

Jezebel will accumulate information secured by becoming close and use it to defame you.

Gossip – *this spirit will visit with you and dine with you for the sole purpose of gossiping. Even pulling together meetings in your name only to criticize you.*

Pride – *this spirit is so prideful that they don't receive counsel or advice from anyone. This spirit is full of justification and can justify every deed and action without ever accepting responsibility. Jezebel refuses to repent even when caught.*

Susceptibility – *this spirit can't stand seeing someone oppose them. They lose their temper easily and keep bitterness in their heart.*

Disobedience – *this spirit does not recognize authority and does not accept being told what to do. In fact, this spirit can't stand being given instructions. In addition, Jezebel can't stand the authority set by God. All advice, reproach and warnings sent by God are rejected.*

Liar – *this spirit is a master at lying. Jezebel can even use different identities to play several roles as a true actor or actress.*

Greed – *this spirt burns with the desire to have more, especially possessions or positions that belong to others. If they can't get it legally, they will get it illegally. This spirit owes debts to brother and sisters with no intention of paying them back.*

Erotomania *– this spirit displays a psychosis or delusion that a person is in love with them, despite contrary evidence. When Jezebel loves someone, and her attentions are not returned she will do everything in her power to destroy them. The person this spirit loves is often superior socially or spiritually. Jezebel suffers from schizophrenia.*

Seductive *– this spirit uses prophecy or the gift of vision to seduce and control their victims. One of the Hebrew translations for seduction is 'nasha' meaning illusion, fantasy. This spirit manipulates feelings. It wraps its victims like a snake and suffocates their ministry without even being noticed. Jezebel will use sweet, flattering words and become your confidante.*

This spirit is deadly.

This spirit targets Christians in earthly and spiritual authority.

"It Took All of That"

135

CHAPTER TEN

"It Took All of That"

As some of you read this book, you're probably thinking it shouldn't take all of that just to get to a place of strength and authority in God. Years ago, I would have agreed with you. I too believed that whatever God wanted out of me He could just sprinkle some magical miracle dust over me and produce it.

Now I know why he says *to whom much is given much is required*. There is a price for the *Anointing*, it costs. There's a price for making a difference in the world. Sacrifices must be made; everyone's sacrifice is different. God never reveals what's required because the truth is if we knew we wouldn't want to make the sacrifice.

It took all of that for this!

"It Took All of That"

My Pastor preached a sermon called "It took All of that" and he shared how he felt like cooking one day and decided to make a sweet potato souffle'.

He talked about how he went to the store to get the ingredients, he got the sweet potatoes and the recipe called for a teaspoon of vanilla extract. He looked all over the store and they were out.

He thought to himself, it's just one tablespoon, it won't make much difference and he kept shopping thinking it don't take all of that.

The recipe called for salted butter and he remembered that he had butter at home, it wasn't salted but it was butter, all the while thinking to himself, it doesn't take all of that. He followed the instructions and at the end it was a beautiful dish. When he tasted it, he realized, it took all of that!

When I look back over my life from my childhood to now, I realize that it took all of that. Honestly, I'm still a work in progress. God is still perfecting me and making me more like Him.

We must watch who we let stand at our gates. Our ear gates, eye gates, all areas of access to us spiritually, mentally and physically.

This is how the Changing of the Guard took place in my life.

Say this prayer with me:

Lord, protect my mind. Sharpen my discernment so that I may see the heart and intentions of those around me. Guard my heart and my spirit from those who desire to pervert your purpose. Expose anyone possessing this spirit.

Amen!

"It Took All of That"

The lightness has turned dark
The truth was just a lie
The cloak of deception
Has been removed and I see you now!

You were never for me
Your words and your actions were enemies
My demise was your desire
You were passionate about it

Relentless, Unyielding even
Tenacious and Determined!
My innocence was stolen
You robbed me of my truth

Your web has entrapped me
Now freedom is sweet
And I am whole again

-   Kasha Hunt

www.ingramcontent.com/pod-product-compliance
Lightning Source LLC
Chambersburg PA
CBHW031851090426
42741CB00005B/442